Genre Drama

Essential Question

When are decisions hard to make?

I0800875

Mixed Messages

by Sharon Holt
illustrated by James Watson

ACT 1

THE WINNER

CHARACTERS

STEVEN and SHEREE (twin brother and sister)

MOM

MR. STRANG (Sheree's teacher)

JASMINE (Sheree's friend)

OTHER STUDENTS

PRINCIPAL GRAY

SCENE 1

Scene: *The kitchen of a suburban home*

STEVEN *and* **SHEREE** *are eating breakfast.*

STEVEN: I hope you sold a lot of cookies. Today's the last day to turn in the money for the **fundraising** contest. We really needed to get money for that new sports equipment.

SHEREE: *(picking up her breakfast dishes)* I'm not good at selling things like you are. You could sell grass to a farmer!

STEVEN: Very funny, but I'm not that good at selling. I just worked hard. I want my class to win the camping trip for selling the most cookies. Don't you want to win the prize for the student who sold the most? I know you like amusement parks.

SHEREE: I don't like amusement parks enough to work that hard.

MOM *enters the room carrying two backpacks.*

MOM: Good morning, kids. I put the money you've raised in your backpacks. Don't forget to hand it in when you get to school.

STEVEN: We were just talking about that money. Sheree was telling me how she was able to sell so many cookies. I wanted her to teach me her brilliant sales **tactics**.

SHEREE: *(picks up her backpack)* Oh, ha, ha.

MOM: Just go brush your teeth, please. The bus will be here soon.

STOP AND CHECK

Why didn't Sheree work hard to sell cookies?

SCENE 2

Scene: *Sheree's classroom*

MR. STRANG *stands at the front of the class.* **SHEREE**, **JASMINE**, *and the* **OTHER STUDENTS** *sit at their desks.*

MR. STRANG: May I have your attention, please? I have an announcement from Principal Gray.

JASMINE: *(whispering to* **SHEREE***)* I hope Mr. Strang is going to say there's no history test today. I forgot to study last night.

MR. STRANG: *(picks up a piece of paper)* Here's Principal Gray's message. "Dear Room 8 students, you will be happy to hear that your class raised an **extensive** amount of money. You raised so much that you won the first prize in the contest."

The class cheers.

MR. STRANG: "The prize is a camping trip for the whole class."

JASMINE: Can we go to Yellowstone Park, Mr. Strang?

MR. STRANG: I haven't finished, Jasmine. *(reading from the paper again)* "There's even more good news. The person who sold the most cookies in the whole school is also from Room 8." Drum roll, please!

SHEREE, **JASMINE**, *and the* **OTHER STUDENTS** *drum on their desks.*

MR. STRANG: The winner of three tickets to Hill Valley Amusement Park is Sheree Bethell!

The class cheers.

SHEREE *looks shocked.*

JASMINE: We won! We won! Roller coasters, here we come!

MR. STRANG: *(raising his hands to get attention)* Be quiet, please.

JASMINE *and the* **OTHER STUDENTS** *settle down.*

MR. STRANG: It's wonderful that you sold so much, Sheree. Stand up and tell us how you did it.

SHEREE *looks around the room.* **JASMINE** *gives her an encouraging smile.*

JASMINE: Say something, Sheree! You should look happy!

SHEREE: *(standing up nervously)* Uh, well, I … I mean, I didn't even … I didn't sell …

MR. STRANG: Come on, Sheree. You should enjoy your success. It's all right to **celebrate** when you've worked hard and reached your goal.

SHEREE: You see, the thing is … I don't really know how … I'm just a little shocked, but thanks anyway.

SHEREE *sits down.*

JASMINE: Mr. Strang, she's just surprised. Her twin brother, Steven, usually wins all the prizes.

MR. STRANG: I understand. Congratulations on doing such a great job, Sheree. Class, our next **endeavor** is to decide where to go for the camping trip.

STOP AND CHECK

Why is Sheree shocked to be named the winner?

ACT 2

AN UNCOMFORTABLE FEELING

SCENE 1

Scene: *The school hallway*

OTHER STUDENTS *are at their lockers.* **SHEREE** *and* **JASMINE** *are talking.*

JASMINE: That was a surprise! I didn't know you sold so many cookies. Aren't you excited?

SHEREE: I'm so confused. I don't know what to do.

JASMINE: Why are you confused? You won! We'll have an awesome time at the amusement park. I hope you want me to come with you.

SHEREE: Of course I do. It's just … *(sighing heavily)*

JASMINE: Everything's great. You worry too much.

SHEREE: You don't understand. There's been a huge mistake.

SHEREE *turns and grabs* **JASMINE** *by the shoulders.*

SHEREE: I can't possibly be the winner. I hardly sold any cookies at all!

JASMINE: *(shocked)* Really? Is that why you were acting so strangely in class?

SHEREE: I guess so. I was just so confused, but now I know what to do. I have to tell Mr. Strang the truth. I'll **confess** right after recess. I'm sure he'll be able to find out who the real winner is.

JASMINE: You can't tell him. You'll disappoint the whole class. Everyone's so excited about the camping trip.

SHEREE: That's why I'm confused. I want to do the right thing, but I don't want to disappoint anyone.

JASMINE: Maybe the right thing is keeping quiet. Just forget about it. No one will ever know.

SHEREE: But I'll know! And it's not right. How would you feel if you had sold all those cookies and someone else got the prize?

JASMINE: *(hands on hips)* You're making this too **complicated**. There's a simple solution—just don't say anything. Now, let's go before someone gets suspicious and thinks we're doing something wrong.

JASMINE *and* **SHEREE** *walk offstage.*

SCENE 2

Scene: *Later in the school hallway*

STEVEN *is standing by the lockers, looking unhappy.* **SHEREE** *and* **JASMINE** *enter.*

JASMINE: What's wrong, Steven?

STEVEN: Our class just found out that we didn't win anything in the contest. I really wanted to go on that camping trip, and I worked so hard.

SHEREE: *(looking sad)* Oh, Steven. I'm really sorry.

STEVEN: It's not your fault. I guess I didn't do as well as I thought.

JASMINE: The good news is our class won the prize!

STEVEN: *(surprised)* Really? That's … great news.

JASMINE: The even better news is that your sister …

SHEREE: *(quickly)* You should get back to class, Steven. You don't want to get detention.

STEVEN *goes offstage.* **MR. STRANG** *comes over to the lockers.*

MR. STRANG: I would like to do some teaching today, girls. That **entails** my students being in their seats.

MR. STRANG *and* **JASMINE** *go offstage.*

SHEREE: *(calling after them)* I'll be right there.

SHEREE *reaches into her backpack and pulls out a paper bag. Her brother's name is on the bag.*

SHEREE: *(to herself)* Oh, no, Mom got the bags mixed up. I handed in Steven's money, and he handed in mine!

STOP AND CHECK

Why doesn't Sheree want Steven to know that she won the prize?

ACT 3

A HARD DECISION

SCENE 1

Scene: *The school auditorium*

SHEREE, **JASMINE**, **STEVEN**, *the* **OTHER STUDENTS**, *and* **MR. STRANG** *are in the audience.* **PRINCIPAL GRAY** *is on the stage.*

PRINCIPAL GRAY: I am so proud of you kids. We made enough money to buy new sports equipment. I'm also **grateful** and would like to thank our **benefactor**, the owner of High Street Sports. He gave an additional $5,000 to our sports teams.

Everyone claps.

PRINCIPAL GRAY: I'm happy to stand here in front of this **multitude** of students and give out the prizes that you've earned. Now, the student who sold the most cookies in the whole school is Sheree Bethell. Please come onto the stage, Sheree.

JASMINE, *the* **OTHER STUDENTS**, *and* **MR. STRANG** *clap.* **STEVEN** *looks shocked.* **SHEREE** *walks onto the stage.*

SHEREE: *(speaking* ***tentatively****)* May I say something, please, Principal Gray?

PRINCIPAL GRAY: *(hands the microphone to* **SHEREE***)* Of course, Sheree.

SHEREE: *(takes a deep breath)* I can't accept this prize. There was a mistake. My bag of cookie money was mixed up with my brother's bag. Steven is the real winner, and he deserves it, too. He worked really hard. I'm sorry for how my **indecision** has affected everyone. I should have known what to do right away.

SHEREE *hands the microphone to* **PRINCIPAL GRAY** *and returns to her seat.*

PRINCIPAL GRAY: Thank you for your honesty, Sheree. It can be very hard to tell the truth sometimes. I'm sure we all have **empathy** for your situation. I am very **impressed** with you and admire how you have handled it.

The **OTHER STUDENTS, STEVEN, JASMINE,** *and* **MR. STRANG** *clap.*

PRINCIPAL GRAY: I have made some quick **calculations** to figure out the winning class. Many other students in Mr. Strang's class sold a lot of cookies. Room 8 is still the winner of the camping trip.

Everyone cheers.

SCENE 2

Scene: *A suburban street*

SHEREE *and* **JASMINE** *are walking home from school.*

JASMINE: I wish we could still go to the amusement park. I was really looking forward to it.

SHEREE: I know, but it would be hard to have fun if I didn't really win.

JASMINE: I don't think I would have been as honest as you were.

SHEREE: I think you would have been honest. Imagine if your little sister had sold all those cookies. Wouldn't you feel bad taking the prize?

JASMINE: I guess so. I wouldn't want to do that to her.

STEVEN: *(running to catch up)* Hey, wait up! I have something to say to you.

SHEREE: I'm sorry, Steven. I should have told the truth sooner.

STEVEN: *(tries to look angry, then smiles)* Don't worry about it. I understand. I'm proud of you for getting up in front of the whole school and explaining what happened. That was brave.

SHEREE: Thanks, Steven. And guess what? I asked Mr. Strang if you could come on the camping trip with our class, and he said yes.

STEVEN: Awesome! I can't wait.

JASMINE: I love when a story has a happy ending!

STEVEN: This one gets even better. Why don't you two take the amusement park tickets? I don't really like amusement parks.

JASMINE: Now, THAT'S what I call a happy ending!

STOP AND CHECK

How do Steven and Sheree end up getting what they wanted?

Respond to Reading

Summarize

Summarize *Mixed Messages*. Use important details from the play. Your graphic organizer may help you.

Detail

↓

Detail

↓

Detail

↓

Theme

Text Evidence

1. What is the theme of this play? What are some clues in Act 2, Scene 1? **THEME**

2. Find the word *confused* on page 8. What clues help you to understand the word's meaning? **VOCABULARY**

3. Write about what happens after Sheree speaks to the school. How do the results show the theme of the play? **WRITE ABOUT READING**

Genre Expository Text

Compare Texts

Read about opera, a form of drama.

What Is Opera?

Did you know that opera began as a short break during plays? Starting in the 1400s, many wealthy Italians enjoyed seeing plays full of drama and sadness. There were musical breaks after each act to give the audience a chance to relax. The audience enjoyed these breaks.

Then poets and musicians had the idea to include music and singing within the plays. Writers and music composers worked together to create a new kind of art. It became known as opera. Opera is an Italian word that means "the work."

Like plays, operas use costumes and scenery.

An opera is a story set to music. It is a mixture of many art forms, including storytelling, singing, and dancing. Operas follow clear plots, just as stories and plays do. Also like stories and plays, the main character in an opera has to solve a problem. Operas can be either serious or funny.

Opera has two main singing styles. In the recitative style, actors sing their dialogue. This keeps the plot moving forward. The aria style has more songs sung by a single singer, called a soloist. Arias stop the action so that people can think about what's happening in the story.

Many people still enjoy traditional operas. However, opera has also changed with the times. In the 1930s, the Gershwin brothers used African American music and jazz in the opera *Porgy and Bess*. The 1950s opera *The Tender Land* is about a teenager during the Great Depression.

Opera has changed even more in recent years. An Australian group called The Ten Tenors mixes opera with modern music. All of these changes are signs that opera is here to stay.

The Ten Tenors sing classical, rock, and pop music.

Make Connections

How are operas like plays? **ESSENTIAL QUESTION**

Plays and operas have characters with problems to solve. Why would *Mixed Messages* work as an opera? **TEXT TO TEXT**

Focus on Genre

Drama In drama, actors act out a story. Forms of drama include plays, films, and puppet shows. An opera is a drama set to music. Plays have a written form called a script. The script shows the actors what to say. It shows them where, when, and how to say their lines.

Read and Find In *Mixed Messages*, on page 2, the script describes the scene and gives stage directions:

Scene 1

Scene: *The kitchen of a suburban home*

STEVEN *and* **SHEREE** *are eating breakfast.*

Your Turn

Work with a small group. Choose one scene from *Mixed Messages*. Reread the scene. Find stage directions that show the scene's place and time. Then discuss how you would design a set for the scene. Think about the painted backdrop behind the actors. A backdrop shows the place where the scene happens. What would you include in the backdrop for your scene? What furniture do the actors need on the stage? What props, or moveable items, will the actors use as they perform the scene?

Share your group's ideas with your class.